Dana's Finger is Set Free
Plus Toolbox
For breaking thumb-sucking habit

Written by Vered Kaminsky

Illustrated by Sara Bat-Or

Dedicated to all the children who are dealing with thumb sucking, and to those who are not, and to all those who contributed to me through their personal experiences, and of course to my Dana.

Dana's Finger is Set Free

Copyright © 2019 by Vered Kaminsky

If you really want to **stop** the thumb-sucking habit, you need to practice. The exercises in **Dana's toolbox** that you can find in the end of the book, will help you break the thumb-sucking habit for good!

When Dana was a baby, she had pacifiers in all kinds of colours,
One pacifier was yellow,
One pacifier was blue,
One pacifier was purple,
One pacifier was red,
And one pacifier was green.
And, if you searched very well, you could also find
a pacifier that changes its colour at night.
But Dana did not want any of these pacifiers,
Dana only wanted her finger.

At the age of six months, it was still cute.
Anyone who saw that tiny baby with a finger
in her mouth would say,
"Such a cute baby, and she already can't take her finger
out of her mouth?"
A year went by, and another, and Dana was much bigger,
and anyone who saw her said,
"Such a big girl, and still with a finger in her mouth?"
But there was no way that Dana would give up
using her finger.
The finger felt warm and dark and sad inside her mouth,
but it could say nothing to Dana,
For you see, fingers cannot talk.

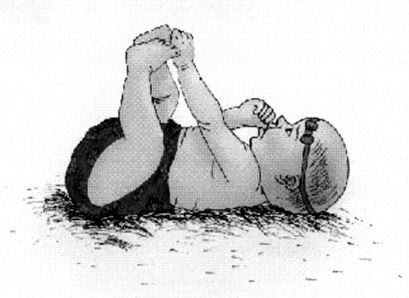

Two more years passed, and Dana was already in kindergarten.
She was considered one of the big kids in that kindergarten.
Her front milk teeth were slightly crooked, and she had a
wrinkled finger with a fractured nail.
And sometimes when the children were assembled in a circle,
she would stick the finger in her mouth when she thought no
one could see.
And so, the days passed by, and Dana continued to put her
finger in her mouth, and nothing helped.
Until one day, her mother decided that Dana was really all grown
up, and the time had come to take her finger out of her mouth -
once and for all.

One Saturday evening, after dinner, Dana's mother called her
and gave her a big sheet of paper with rows and letters and said,
"Here is a mission: stop using your finger as a pacifier until next
Saturday."
Dana looked at her mother and asked,
"How? This is so hard to do."
"At first, try during assembly in the kindergarten.
Then, try while watching TV or playing.
Then during the whole day, and finally, even during the night."
Dana picked up the chart in which there were many rows and
seemed alarmed.
Her mother saw her alarmed expression, and she smiled and said,
"Every day that passes without your finger in your mouth,
You will put a sticker on the chart – just like the one the
kindergarten teacher gives children who behave well.
If you succeed – you will get a special gift."

Dana picked up the chart and went to her room.

She sat on her bed and thought to herself,

"What will I do now? How do I stop?"

And while she was thinking, she stuck her finger into her mouth again.

"I will think about it tomorrow", she promised herself.

And she put the big chart under her pillow and fell asleep.

The next morning, she took out the chart, which was slightly crumpled, looked over the empty columns and decided to start on her mission.

But it was not easy at all.

On the first day, Dana tried not to stick her finger in her mouth, but a few times she found it in her mouth without even realizing it.

And when her mother accidentally passed by and saw it, she smiled and said, "I trust you Dana. You can do it."

And Dana knew that her finger was inside her mouth again.

"How will I manage to stop this habit?" she thought to herself,
"It is so hard…"

Sadly, she looked at her wrinkled finger and the cracked nail,
and one big tear dropped on her finger.

Suddenly, she had an idea.

She went to the drawer in her desk, took out a glowing red
marker, and drew a smiley on her finger.

Dana believed that each time she almost stuck her finger in
her mouth, the smiley would smile at her even more.

And so, at the very last minute, the finger would remain
outside of her mouth.

A few times, she did not manage to stop in time.

The finger got into her mouth, and the smiley was erased or
became crooked.

But gradually, the finger remained outside more and more,
until it stopped getting into her mouth by itself at all.

Each day that went by without her finger in her mouth,
Dana placed a sticker on the chart and drew a smiley on it.
On Sunday, Monday and Tuesday, when she occasionally
found her finger in her mouth, she drew half a smiley on
the sticker.
Then on Wednesday, Thursday and Friday,
she drew only smileys.

On Saturday morning, Dana woke up early, looked at her finger and noticed that it had straightened out, and the nail was not so cracked.

She picked up the chart and went to wake up her mother.

"Mommy," she said almost whispering, "I've succeeded!"

Mother picked up the chart, looked at it and said,

"My sweet Dana, kudos to you! You see? You really wanted to succeed, and you did."

Dana's mother promised to buy her any gift of her choice.

Dana kept thinking all that day about what she wanted.

She was excited and looked at the finger with the smiley – and she smiled back.

The next day, they both went to the toy shop, and Dana chose a doll she had wanted for a long time.

And so, after six years inside her mouth,
wrinkled and with a cracked nail,
Dana's finger was set free.

Finally, her finger was set free,
to play, to paint and to do
whatever fingers do.

Now, Dana is in first grade, and the days of
having a finger in her mouth are over.
But, sometimes, only sometimes, when Dana's
mother comes quietly, quietly into her room in
order to tuck her in, she realizes that before
Dana fell asleep, she drew the red smiley again,
and it seems that Dana is smiling back at it.

Dear Parents,

We are glad that you have joined us on the mutual journey of weaning your child from the thumb-sucking habit. As we know, initially, thumb sucking appears and develops in the fetus – namely, in the mother's womb.

Some children continue this behavior even after birth. Sucking the thumb turns into their remedy for tiredness, fear, bore-dom and illness, or as a way of dealing with an adaptation period they are going through, for exam-ple the first day at a new school, moving to another apartment in another city, etc.

The weaning process is necessary, essential and im-portant, since the thumb-sucking habit interferes with the child's daily life and affects all areas of life. This action disconnects him/her from society and causes him/her to be ashamed of the habit or even become ostracized and considered a "baby", and all this without even mentioning the medical problems that accompany the phenomenon.

Parents describe difficulty with the habit's effects and express a desire to stop it.

Thumb sucking is not just something children do – there are testimonies of adults who claim that this habit does not stop at an older age. Some suck their thumb to fall asleep or when they feel angry and nervous. This goes to show that it is an annoying habit at any age. It is important to remember that the desire to stop this habit must come from the child himself/herself, in order for the process to succeed! That is why, before you begin the weaning process with the help of our digital course, you must check if your child is ready and willing to start the process.

In addition, for the process to achieve the best results, it is recommended that adults be present and involved in the process, as well as provide positive and empowering feedback. It is also recommended to share with the other members of the family the process that this specific child is going through.

The success of any weaning process depends not only on the child himself/herself, but also on his/her environment. So, if you really want your child to be weaned of the habit of sucking on a finger, it is recommended to accompany him/her throughout the process.

* The strategies are based on a behavioral coaching model developed by Lisa Grossman, M.Ed., MA., Educational Psychologist and ADHD Coach, that enables adults working with children to create practical plans for changing habits in every area of life.

Dana's Toolbox
For breaking thumb-sucking habit

Hi, I really hope you liked the book: 'Dana's Finger Is Set Free'.

If you really want to stop the thumb sucking habit,
you need to practice.
The practice exercises in Dana's toolbox will help you
break the thumb sucking habit for good!

What is a toolbox?

A toolbox is a kit with strategies to help change behavior.
Dana's toolbox includes questions, suggestions and charts that will
give you tools for success. **It is important** to start with the strategies,
and then when you feel ready, you can start to fill in Dana's chart.

> This plan works best for children above 4 years old, and the
> Adults' guidance is needed to follow each strategy, step by step.

Are you ready? Let's begin!

Before we begin please answer **yes or no:**

Do you **want** to stop the thumb sucking habit? _____ !

Are you **ready to work** hard to stop the thumb sucking habit? _____ !

My Goal

First, write your goal: For example, "My goal is to stop sucking my thumb as soon as..."

_____

_____

What do you need to do in order to achieve your goal?
For example, to be more aware, to find other things to do instead of sucking my thumb, to ask an adult to remind me..."

_____

_____

Who can help you achieve your goal?

_____

_____

Why is achieving this goal important to you?

_____

_____

How will breaking this habit help you?

_____

_____

What might prevent you from achieving your goal?

_____

_____

When would you like to start achieving your goal?

_____

_____

What are some "baby steps" that you can take to help you succeed?
For example, on the first day, I can stop sucking my thumb for a few hours, then for...

_____

_____

How will you feel after you have reached your goal?

_____

_____

How will you feel if you don't reach your goal?

_____

_____

What positive words from your parents will help you reach your goal? (Such as – "I know it is hard, but I believe you can do it!" – or: "Way to go!!")

_____

_____

What rewards might help you stay focused on your goal?
For example, special privileges, fun activities such as going to the movies, sleeping at a friend's house...

_____

_____

What positive thoughts might help you when you get stuck and want to give up?

_____

_____

Values

Values are like a compass that guide us in making choices based on what is important to us. Values such as..., friendship, learning, self-discipline, independence and creativity, give meaning to our lives and serve as goals for improving ourselves. Values keep us focused, so that we do not give up until we have achieved our goals. We feel truly fulfilled, when we live according to our values.

What values will become stronger when I work on breaking the thumb sucking habit?

**Circle values that are connected
to breaking the thumb sucking habit**

happiness	**success**	**effort**
self-confidence	**pleasure**	**growing up**
letting go	**self-awareness**	**discipline**
being responsible	**humor**	**hope**

Imagine

Imagine a movie called:

_____

The movie is about you, going through the steps that you wrote down in the goal- setting page. Begin with the first step, and imagine yourself moving each step forward, until you finally succeed.

What will you be doing differently? How will you feel about yourself? What will you be able to do successfully after you have broken this habit? What are others saying about you? Imagine that you are helping somebody else with the thumb sucking habit, by telling him your story.

Write your story here:

_____

_____

_____

_____

_____

But watch out!!

There is an Elf in your mind!

Did you know?

There is a small but powerful elf in your mind and in everybody's mind!
This elf tries to control your mind and convince you that you won't succeed.
The elf usually looks sweet and harmless but be careful! That's only because he wants you to listen to him and do what he says!
The thumb sucking elf will say - "its nice sucking a finger" – "don't listen to anyone" - "You won't ruin your teeth, so why stop?"

GUESS WHAT?
YOU CAN TAME YOUR ELF!

How?

✓ NOTICE WHEN YOUR ELF IS SPEAKING TO YOU.

✓ RECOGNIZE THAT THE ELF WANTS YOU TO FAIL.

✓ USE YOUR AFFIRMATIONS FOLLOWING THE NEXT
   PART, AND TALK BACK TO YOUR ELF.

Elf taming exercise
This exercise will help you tame your elf:

CLOSE YOUR EYES AND IMAGINE YOUR ELF SITTING SOMEWHERE IN YOUR BODY.

WHAT DOES YOUR ELF LOOKS LIKE?

WHERE IN YOUR BODY DOES YOUR ELF SIT?

IN YOUR HEAD? ON YOUR SHOULDER? IN YOUR EAR?

WHAT IS HE WHISPERING TO YOU?

WHAT DOES HE WANT?

HOW WILL YOU FEEL WHEN YOU SUCCESSFULLY TAME YOUR ELF?

NOW THAT YOU KNOW ME BETTER YOU CAN EASILY TAME ME!

Affirmations

Affirmations are positive sentences that people say to themselves to help them control behavior and do their best to succeed. Here is a list of **affirmations** that you can use to build a positive mind set:

> **I am strong!**

> **I am smart enough to handle anything!**

> **I am creative!**

> **I believe in myself!**

> **I know how to ask for help if I need it!**

> **I know my abilities and I keep improving them!**

> **I use my sense of humor!**

> **I know that the ball is in my hand!**

> **I NEVER give up!!!**

Add your own affirmations here!

_____

_____

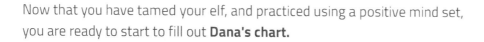

You are one step away from achieving your goal!!!

Now that you have tamed your elf, and practiced using a positive mind set,
you are ready to start to fill out **Dana's chart.**

Instructions for filling out the chart:

Put a smiley face on each day that passes without any thumb sucking.
Place half a smiley face on days that you had some thumb sucking, but not as much as before.
Place a thinking smiley face on a day that you didn't succeed at all.
Try again tomorrow! you will succeed!

If you feel like you need some help, you can read over the exercises and imagine
the movie that you made up.

Remember!
"If you can imagine it, you can do it!"
Walt Disney

After 2 weeks of successfully
following the program, you will
reach your goal, just like Dana did!

Creative

Color the Elf & Dana
in your own colors

Dana's Chart

Get rid of the thumb sucking habit easily

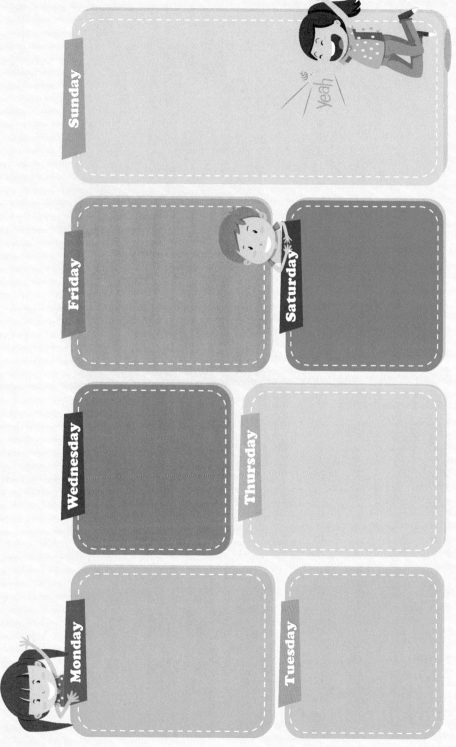

Sunday

Friday

Saturday

Wednesday

Thursday

Monday

Tuesday

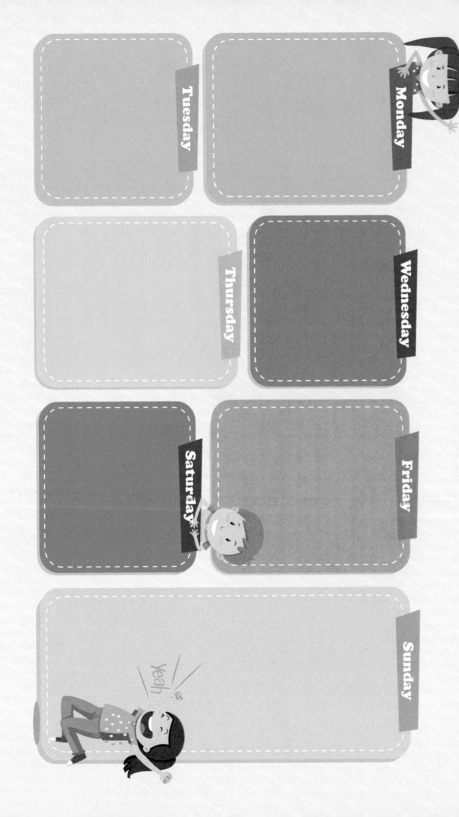

Dana's Chart

Get rid of the thumb sucking habit easily

Monday

Tuesday

Wednesday

Thursday

Friday

Saturday

Sunday

Dana's Chart

Get rid of the thumb sucking habit easily

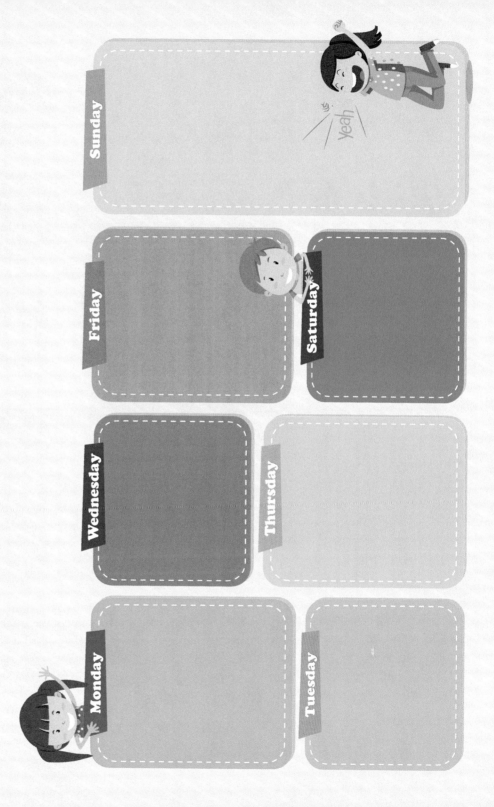

Sunday

Friday

Saturday

Wednesday

Thursday

Monday

Tuesday

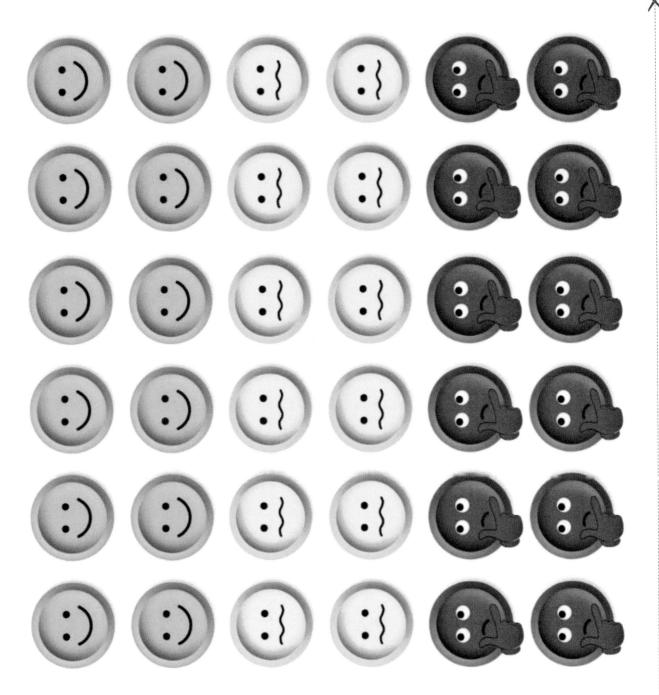

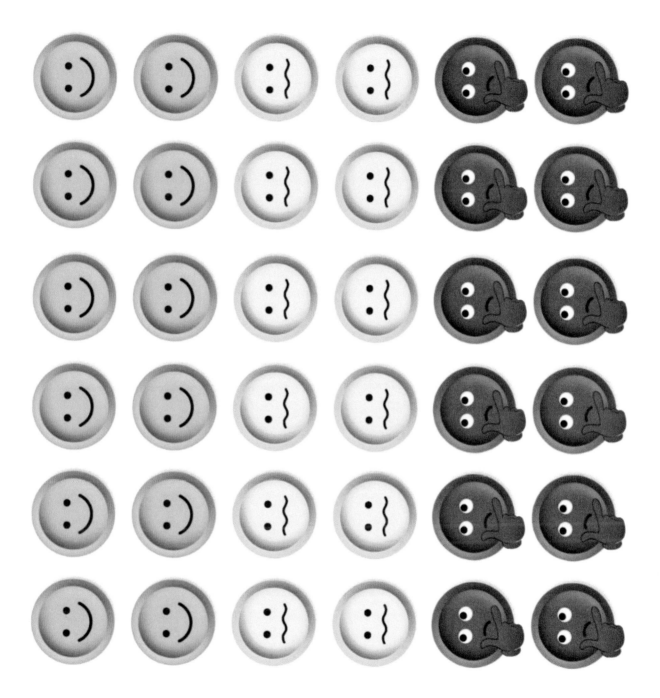

Thank you for reading "Dana's Finger Is Set Free".
If you want to get more activities pages
and get rid of your thumb-sucking habit,
Please send us an email to:

info@epos.co.il

And we will send you the chart as a reply.

Help your child get rid of the thumb-sucking habit, with the
digital course that you can find at the link below:

http://bit.ly/2J9yDAi

Made in the USA
Middletown, DE
19 October 2022

13127232R00027